An Introduction to

BUSINESS

For

AFRICAN-AMERICAN

YOUTH

An Introduction to

BUSINESS

for

AFRICAN-
AMERICAN

YOUTH

ABNER MCWHORTER

XPRESSION PUBLISHING
453 MARTIN LUTHER KING BLVD.
DETROIT, MI 48201

For my daughter, Zuri McWhorter whose life is my inspiration.

Editing by Debra Adams
Illustrations by Shelby McPherson
Art Direction by Russell Bailey

First Edition: March 1995

"An Introduction to Business for African-American
Youth"/ Abner McWhorter. - 1st Edition
ISBN 0-9645840-1-8 (pbk.)

Library of Congress Catalog Card Number: 95-60607.

For further information write to:

Xpression Publishing
453 Martin Luther King Blvd.
Detroit, MI 48201

TABLE OF CONTENTS

ACKNOWLEDGMENTS

As a business owner, I take great pride in the fact that I have accomplished many things on my own. However, this book is not one of them. It required a great deal of patience and support to complete such an important project. I would like to thank those who have been inspirational and helpful.

My endless appreciation to my mother, Sharon McWhorter, whose entrepreneurial spirit was passed on to me; Josie Aaron, my grandmother, who provides a place of refuge through her unconditional love and support; Abner McWhorter II, my father, for the discipline you instilled early in my life; Bill Stewart, whose brilliance has exposed the world to me and given me a foundation to build upon; Glenn Oliver, my lawyer and business partner, who provides remarkable business savvy, astute legal skills and an abundance of enthusiasm; my uncle, Lonnie Ervin, who has unselfishly given advice and support throughout the years; Debra Adams, whose dedication and editing skills has improved this book immeasurably; Marian Dozier who's input helped complete this project; my uncle, Gus Richards, who put his money were his mouth is and gave me my first loan at age 16 and Arthur and Larrie Bates, my gratitude for welcoming me into your family unconditionally. To all my friends and staff who helped lessen burdens both financially and socially, Jonathan Simmons, Russell Bailey, Cheryl Bates, Erica Bates, Carol Varner and Joe Richardson.

Most of all, I am thankful to my partner, Beverly Bates, whose contribution to this book is outweighed only by her contributions to my life.

A MESSAGE TO PARENTS

It is with great pleasure that this book is written. All parents want success and prosperity for their children. There are many avenues in attaining these goals. Successful business ownership can be one of the most personally and financially rewarding choices. This book is our attempt to help you instruct your children on how to start a business for themselves by offering a step-by-step guide to entrepreneurial opportunities for children ages 8 to 18.

Remember, it wasn't so long ago that you dreamed of owning your own business and accomplishing the great American dream. Too many of our children have succumbed to the great American nightmares of illiteracy, delinquency, drug abuse, drug selling, crime and more. This book does not hold the answers to these ills, however it can offer positive choices for African-American children. Our communities need more young African-American entrepreneurs establishing and maintaining profitable businesses.

Although each business has been carefully selected, parental supervision is required. Your involvement will create a safe business environment for your child, as well as provide you with information on how to start and run a business of your own. Obtaining economic freedom is the next challenge for African Americans. In many ways our success or failure at achieving that goal will depend on our youth. It is my hope that this book will help train our next generation of entrepreneurs.

ABOUT THE AUTHOR

Abner McWhorter began his first business venture at age eleven, selling candy at school. It occurred to him that if he could sell candy profitably for the school band, he could do the same for himself. He learned very early how to negotiate with wholesalers and create a demand for his product. Mastering the art of candy selling in both middle and high school provided him with income ten times his initial investment in merchandise.

McWhorter has worked hard as a student of the school of self-employment. Realizing that candy sales were limited, he began a grass-cutting business, called Dr. Lawn Care. Although he was under the legal age for driving, he solved his transportation problems by hiring workers old enough to drive and renting his mother's van and lawn mower. Again, his landscaping business was successful due to his innovative marketing skills such as servicing customers in affluent neighborhoods.

By the time McWhorter was sixteen, he was the youngest partner in a retail operation called The Donut Man, which sold novelty mini-donuts and beverages. The business was located in the food court of downtown Detroit's largest mall . This endeavor further developed his negotiating skills. He and his partners were responsible for seven employees working three shifts, seven days a week. Oddly enough, everyone involved with the business - including the employees - were older than McWhorter, who was managing sales in excess of $1,000 a weekend.

McWhorter, realizing the limitations of his current business, sought out a product that was marketable to both individuals and corporations. Remembering a neighbor who had considerable success providing custom framing services, it occurred to McWhorter that this business provided the customer base and the growth potential he was looking for. With a small loan from his uncle, McWhorter began his own picture framing business, called Frame Up. At the ripe old age of seventeen, McWhorter's business venture, which did not interrupt his school obligations, generated gross sales in excess of $150,000 in the second year of operation. As sales continued to grow McWhorter was able to open a second retail store in downtown Detroit's financial district and was eventually awarded the city's art and engineering supply contract.

McWhorter now concentrates on expanding his business and lecturing across the country on the benefits of youth entrepreneurship. He knows the obstacles awaiting people interested in starting their own business and hopes this book will provide information, ideas and encouragement to anyone interested in financial independence.

ABSTRACT JEWELRY

This type of jewelry is called abstract because you have the freedom to use just about everything to create it. Broken album and puzzle pieces, newspapers and old photos make unique and uncommon pieces of jewelry.

HOW TO GET STARTED

Abstract jewelry is best made into earrings and pins because it can be too bulky for necklaces or bracelets. The idea is to use each piece to create something unique or with a popular theme. For example, you can affix your own drawings or images from newspapers, magazines and comics to the back of puzzle pieces. Mat board (thin rigid board found in art supply stores) or broken album pieces can also be used for backing. The jewelry pieces can be finished over with a gloss from an arts and crafts store to give the jewelry a shiny look. If you are unfamiliar with this technique, don't worry. Instructions on glossing should be included or ask a salesperson. If you are making pins, you want to secure a jewelry locking pin to the back of your creation. For clip earrings, you can stick the clip to the back of the earring just as you would do with the pins. Make sure that you use glue that will not irritate skin.

Again, your local arts and crafts store should be able to
help you with this. For pierced earrings, put a small hole at
the top of your image and backing. Insert either a fish line
or thin but durable thread into the small hole. Tie fish line
or thread at both ends. There should be at least one inch between the pierced ear clip and the backing. You can also
add decorative beads to the fish line or thread for flair. Be
creative! Anything from ethnic fabric to images of political
movements can be used to create abstract jewelry.

SUPPLIES

Broken Album Pieces (ask permission first)
Earring Backings (clip-on and pierced)
Backings for Pins (puzzle pieces or mat board)
Glue (ask at arts and crafts store for best type)

Gloss (ask at arts and crafts store for best type)
Images from newspapers, magazines, drawings, etc.

MARKETING

Marketing an abstract jewelry business starts off with word of mouth, but you should also read the local newspapers for flea markets or shows where you can rent a booth and sell your jewelry. If you try this route, find out as much information as you can about the demographics and size of the crowd that usually attends the event. This will help determine what type of jewelry to bring and how much. As always, fliers can help you get customers. Remember, they must always look professional!

PRICING

This is up to you, but remember to include the cost of your labor and the cost of your materials. You should also remember that your creations are unique and one-of-a-kind, when setting your price. However, you don't want to price yourself out of the market; check around at flea markets, festivals, speciality shops and boutiques to get an idea of the price range for similar items.

UNDERSTANDING THE STOCK MARKET

An open forum where people, using a broker, can become part owners of a company by purchasing SHARES of stock. If the company does well, you earn money, if it doesn't you lose money!

52-week High	52-week Low	Stock	Div.	Yld.	PE	Sales 100's	High	Low	Last	Chg.
16	10	ACToy	.45	3.9	13	303	14	12	13	-1

This shows the highest and lowest price of each share of stock paid within the last 52 weeks.

This is a SYMBOL. It is an abbreviation of the company listed. Example "ACToy" stands for Americo Toy Co.. There are books that can help you with this at the library.

A DIVIDEND is paid by some companies as an extra incentive to buy their stock. This is a sharing of the profits. For example .45 is 45 cents. You would get this amount every year for each SHARE of stock you own.

A YIELD is the rate of interest being paid on the stock by the dividend. Example: If you buy a share of stock for $5 each share and you get a Dividend of 35 cents, then your YIELD is 7 or 7%.

PRICE/EARNING RATIO is a rating of the past performance, yield on dividend and sales of shares on stock exchange. This column is mostly used by brokers.

The SALES 100's is the number of shares, times one hundred, sold that day on the stock exchange. For example if the number is 91 it means 9,100 shares were sold.

HIGH AND LOW tells the highest and lowest price paid for of each share of stock that day. LAST tells the price of the stock when the market closed that day.

CHANGE tells the difference in the price of the stock from the day before.

Reginald F. Lewis

Before his untimely death in January 1993, Reginald F. Lewis was chairman and C.E.O. of the largest African-American business in the U.S. With annual sales in excess of $1.8 billion, TLC Beatrice International is truly a world-class enterprise.   Under the leadership of Lewis' widow, Loida Picolas Lewis, the company still operates plants and offices throughout Europe.

In 1992, Lewis was the first African American to have a building named after him at Harvard Law School. Through his foundation, Lewis gave over $12 million to a variety of causes. In 1994, a biography of his life, **"Why Should White Guys Have All The Fun?"** became a Best-Seller.

AQUARIUM CLEANING & MAINTENANCE

Many people and businesses own aquariums, however most people don't like to clean them because it can take a great deal of time. The water temperature has to be carefully maintained. The fish have to be housed elsewhere temporarily. The tank and its components have to be cleaned and rinsed. This job will make most aquarium owners tired just thinking about it. However, if you like live fish, water creatures and plants, this business could provide plenty of revenue. Everything you need to start this business is readily available at your local pet shop or large variety store. Start-up costs are well under $150. Depending on the number of customers you service, your earning potential could certainly exceed $150 monthly.

HOW TO GET STARTED

Talk to pet store owners/managers and ask them who cleans their aquariums and how much they charge. This information will help you set prices and determine the best hours to work. If you have never owned an aquarium, you may want to monitor a few cleanings at friends' houses or a pet store. Detail the type of fish, plants and water - salt or fresh - how they are transferred from one tank to another while cleaning and how long the entire cleaning takes. Because of the careful handling required, especially with salt water fish and plants, you will need to learn about aquariums and the care of water pets. Remember, your local library has books to provide you with the information you need to get started.

MARKETING

Initial customers may be pet store owners, however don't overlook relatives and friends. Most of your sales and marketing can be done through fliers posted at libraries, supermarkets, local churches, local block club newsletters or newspaper classified sections. In addition, many colleges and universities have local newsletters to place your ads in and boards to post your fliers. Don't forget to list the best time to call and some of your prices. Try to offer a bonus of some sort to promote using your services, such as free algae eater with every 10-gallon cleaning or free colored gravel with every 20-gallon cleaning.

If you enjoy working with small, caged pets, you might want to extend your services to general cage and aquarium cleaning. Fish are not the only species living in aquariums.

If you are not afraid of lizards, gerbils, snakes, etc., you can further capitalize on this business endeavor. Cleaning a terrarium or cage is a service that generally requires removing animal droppings and cleaning or replacing of soil, wood chips, etc. Before starting a cage and terrarium cleaning business be sure to know the complete background of the particular animal you are handling. Pet stores might want you to clean up more than the fish aquariums. Offer these services to all prospective customers and expand your services when practical.

PRICING

Prices can be determined by calling your competitors and asking how much they charge per gallon. You will also want to ask if there is an additional charge for coming to a customers' home or office. This information will help you stay competitive. Furthermore, pet stores can provide the same information on the companies they use to clean their aquariums. Most business owners want to save money, so if you offer the same reliable service at a more reasonable price, they will want your services. Basically, you will price your services based on the size of the tank and the number of fish to be cared for.

EQUIPMENT & SUPPLIES

Wet and Dry Vacuum
5 Gallon Holding Aquarium
Thermostats
Nets and Brushes
Cleaning Tablets and Agents

Plastic Pails
Plastic Drop Cloths
Sponge Mop

INVENTORY

Inventory is the resaleable goods available in stock. Managing inventory is a very sensitive area within any merchandising business. You can have too little or too much. "Stock Outs" is a term used when a

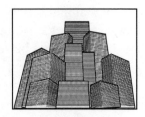

business does not have the merchandise on hand to sell to the consumer. In most cases the customer will not wait around for you to re-order the product you should already have. The result is that you lose the potential sale and may develop a reputation for not being able to service your clients. Based on the above, it would seem like you could never have too much inventory, but you can. When a business sinks too much cash into its inventory, it restricts itself from having money on hand for basic operating expenses. You find yourself with ample product and no money to pay bills.

One way to control this problem is to date items when you buy them. Then set time limits on how long you keep them. For instance, if a product does not sell within 90 days, you may consider selling it at a discount to get your cash out of the item. Keep in mind, it is not a good idea to buy this particular product again. Use this money for buying faster-selling merchandise. With any type of product you carry, you want to turn it into cash as soon as possible by selling it to a customer.

Don H. Barden

HBO, Showtime, Cinemax and of course, MTV- Barden Cablevision brought these and more cable networks into the homes of Detroiters in 1983 when it was awarded the cable franchise for Detroit, Michigan.

However, Barden Cablevision is only a piece of The Barden Companies, Inc., whose Chief Executive Officer Don H. Barden began his career with a retail record outlet at the age of 21.

His business career has spanned 25 years. Barden has guided his company from annual revenues of $600,000 to over $90 million in 11 years. In 1994, The Barden Companies, Inc., which operates in the broadcasting, real estate development as well as entertainment industries, was ranked 13th largest black-owned business in the U. S.

BABY-SITTING

Being a parent is a beautiful experience, yet it is also a full-time job that leaves parents with little time for anything else. Parents value responsible, attentive and loving babysitters who will look after their children with the same care and devotion they would.

If you like children and are responsible and patient, maybe becoming an on-call or temporary child care provider is the business for you. There is hardly a shortage of babysitters around, so the key is to present your service as different and superior to the rest.

HOW TO GET STARTED

To excel in this business, you have to make yourself stand out. Develop a babysitting kit, by putting together a collection of educational toys, quizzes and books. Also, bring old clothing with you to play dress-up. This game not only helps children learn to dress themselves, it also helps them learn colors. There is nothing worse than sitting a child in front of the television while the baby-sitter talks on the phone. Think about it. If parents come home and their child tells them something they have learned from you instead of what was on television, you will be viewed as an asset to the parent. Remember, anybody can sit and watch a child. It is a unique, patient and caring individual who is willing to interact with the child and to teach him/her while making it all fun! It seems like a lot of work, but if you enjoy children, the time will fly by. Keep in mind that children love attention. By providing them with this attention you will become their friend and they will continue to ask for you when their parents need a sitter.

There are some rules you must follow when babysitting. If the child is in diapers, make sure you change the diaper often, clean the child thoroughly and dispose of the diaper properly. Always follow the schedule left for the children by the parents. For example, put the children to bed and feed them at the specified times. Serve the food that the parents have left for them. To avoid any allergic reactions or disapproval from the parents, don't give the children any food surprises unless you ask parents first. Always have a telephone number where you can reach the parents or a neighbor they trust in case of an emergency. It is also a good practice to be in contact with your own parents and give them the number where you are; you may need to call them for advice. Of course, you should know the phone number to the fire and police departments. When answering the telephone, never let the person on the other end know that you are alone with the children. Tell them that the person they asked for cannot come to the phone and will return their call.

Make sure you are well rested before going to your job. Being trustworthy means not sleeping when you should be watching the children, even when they are asleep. Clean up any mess that you and the children make. Leave the house just as it was when you arrived. Do not have any company and try not to talk on the phone. If you are there during din-

ner, lunch or even breakfast, bring your own food unless the parents have given you permission to eat with the children. And of course, you should never use any household equipment (computers, stereo, appliances, car, etc.) unless given permission by the parents.

You may also want to go above and beyond the call of duty by offering to wash dishes, or put something back where it belongs without charging for this service. This will be viewed as another incentive to hire you. Doing more and doing less is always noticed. There is no room for mediocrity and you definitely do not want to do less than expected!

If business is going well, it may be a good idea to purchase games and activities for different age groups. If your business is booming, you should consider hiring and training other responsible friends to send out on babysitting jobs.

However, you will be responsible for what they do and how they behave, so you must be sure that the people you hire are as professional as you are.

Another aspect of the babysitting business would be Saturday-only services. Working parents tend to cram all their chores into one day, and that is usually Saturday. Often, they can get much more accomplished without the children. With your parents' permission you could offer parents the option of dropping off the children at your house. If there are events for children on Saturdays, you may offer to take them there. This will get the children out of the house and give them something fun and interesting to do while the parents take care of their business.

Baby-sitting is probably one of the most fun and adventurous jobs you can have. The one thing to remember is that although you want to get paid for providing quality care for children, money cannot be your primary motive. It is a business that you have to love which requires patience, devotion, creativity and most importantly, maturity.

SUPPLIES

Games
Toys
Snacks (with parents permission)
Puzzles
Coloring Books and Crayons

MARKETING

Although there are a lot of people willing to babysit, parents are looking for someone they can trust. After all, they will be leaving their most precious possession in the care of someone else and they need to feel confident that they have chosen the right person.

It is part of your job to make prospective customers feel confident about you. You can start with your own parents, asking them to inform friends and co-workers that you are available to provide child care. If you live in an apartment or co-op, post fliers that are professional and honest. Make members of your church or community group aware of your service. As stated before, parents need to feel comfortable with their choice, so offer to interview with the parents and children before taking the job. This will help you and the parents know if you are right for the task of caring for their children.

Offer standing dates as part of your service. For instance, you may have a customer who goes to the gym every Wednesday from 6:30pm-8:30pm. Let them know that you could be available for babysitting at that time. This would be a great opportunity because you may schedule as many standing dates as you have time for and still maintain the other responsibilities you may have. You may want to take pictures while playing with the children. For instance, if you play dress up, snap a picture and leave it at their home or mail it to the parents with a thank-you note for using your service. This professionalism will produce both money and high respect for the quality of your service.

PRICING

The most important thing is to figure what parents want and how much you are going to charge for it. You should check around to find out what the standard rate is for straight baby-sitting. Once you know that, then you can set a price for any special services your customer may want. It would be a good idea to figure out how many children you will be babysitting and come up with a price per child. Also, you will need to know if you'll be required to prepare meals, give baths or dress the children for bed. Make sure that you clearly establish this with the parents beforehand.

TAXES

Every business has a silent partner,
Uncle Sam. That's right, the government also shares in the profit of your
money-making venture. Depending
on what business you operate, you may be liable for taxes
to city, state and federal authorities. All levels of government will require you to report and collect taxes for any employee you pay $600 or more in a year. If you don't have
the need for full-time employees, you may want to make
them "independent contractors," which means they are not
employees of your company. In that case, they must fill out
a 1099 form which makes them responsible for their own
taxes. If your business makes an annual profit of $400 or
more, you will need to file a Schedule C form at the end of
the year. You can get both of these forms from the Federal
government's Internal Revenue Service.

If you sell products that have sales taxes applied to them,
you must report and pay a percentage of your products' selling price (rates vary state to state). Contact your state's Department of Treasury to determine if your business is
required to collect sales taxes. City governments usually
tax based on the value of a company's assets. This is usually a minimal fee, but you must make sure that it is paid.

Don't be intimidated by these responsibilities. There are
professionals such as accountants and bookkeepers that can
help you. These professionals do charge a fee for their service, but for a young person starting out it shouldn't be too
expensive.

BASEMENT, ATTIC AND GARAGE CLEANING AND SALES

Cleaning the basement, attic or garage has been a dreaded chore for as long as they have existed. People know it has to be done but they put it off, adding more and more to the mountain of "junk" they have accumulated. This dread of cleaning out basements, garages and attics could ultimately turn into profits for you. There are two parts to this business. First, the actual cleaning of these spaces. Second, getting your customers' permission to use some of the items you remove for your own garage sale.

HOW TO GET STARTED

Decide whether you will simply remove the unwanted items in these areas or if your service will include actual cleaning, such as mopping, dusting and sweeping. Keep in mind that some jobs may require more than one day's work and you may need to hire a helper. Therefore, it is important for you to see the place you will be cleaning beforehand and set a realistic timetable for completing the job.

While talking with your prospective customers, it would be a good idea to introduce the second part of your business - the Garage Sale. Ask your customers if they would be willing to let you take some things for your garage sale. Be honest. Don't say you just want them for yourself. Nothing would be worse than for them to stop by your sale and see some things from their home. If the customer doesn't want to give you the items, then offer to pay for them. Five dollars would probably be better to them than nothing. Once you have the items you can then set your prices, based on your cost, at your garage sale.

EQUIPMENT & SUPPLIES

Mops
Brooms

Dust Mops
Cleaning Solutions
Boxes
Gloves
Hand Truck

MARKETING

The first and most obvious place to begin is at home. Most likely, your parents will be supportive if they know you are serious about starting a business. Starting at home will help them out and allow you to get an idea of how long such jobs take.

 The next place to go would be to older relatives and neighbors. Elderly people tend to keep lots of things and are probably not going to attempt a major project like this. You would be a great help to them.

Another idea for customers would be helping people move into or out of homes. Often when people move, they are swamped and would welcome the assistance. It would also give you the opportunity to remove items left by previous occupants. Look around the neighborhood for "For Sale" signs and simply approach the person moving. You should also consider going to real estate agencies to seek out individuals who may be moving. As always, be prepared with your flier!

BOOKKEEPING
MANAGING YOUR MONEY

Bookkeeping can be one of
the most neglected tasks in
a business, but probably one
of the most important.

Here's a simple way to get
started. Get twenty-four manila folders or large envelopes to store your receipts. Mark twelve *Income* and the
other twelve *Expenses*. Mark each with a month's name.
If you start your business in February 1995, then mark
your first set of folders or envelopes "*Income Feb. 1995*"
and "*Expenses Feb. 1995*" followed by the next 11
months until your last set, which should be Jan. 1996.

Whenever you receive money for your business, give
your customer a receipt or an invoice and keep a copy for
your **income** folder for that specific month. Use two receipts with a carbon between them. Copy and use the
sample invoice in the "Forms" section of this book or get
ready-made, pre-numbered invoices at most office supply
stores. If using invoices in the back of this book, make
sure to assign different invoice numbers for each transaction.

Also, get a receipt whenever you buy goods or services
for your business. With each receipt, attach a purchase

Bookkeeping Cont.

order slip. The purchase order describes the purchase. This form will help control spending. Purchase orders are also in the "Forms" section of this book. Again, assign different purchase order numbers for each transaction. Place purchase orders and expense receipts in the **expense** folder in the specific month the purchase was made.

At the end of each month, list all transactions on an **Income** and **Expense Journal** sheet. These forms can also be found in the "Forms" section of this book. You should have one Expense and Income Journal sheet for every expense and income file, dated for that specific month. At the end of the month total all your income receipts on your Income Journal and all of your purchase orders on your Expense Journal.

Then, transfer these totals to a **Profit and Loss Statement**, commonly known as a P&L. This form simply tells you how much money you've made or lost. This form is also in the back of the book.

Don't put this very important part of your business off. This process sounds a lot more difficult than it really is. It just takes a little practice and you will get the hang of it in no time. Remember, making money is one of the most important parts of a business. Keeping track of it is just as important.

CALLIGRAPHY

Calligraphy is defined as the art of beautiful writing. By mastering this art you can produce magnificent script and earn a profit. Calligraphy is a skill that can be learned by anyone whether 11 or 111 years old, provided you enjoy writing and working with your hands.

HOW TO GET STARTED

This skill's major requirement is your time, not money. Start-up cost are under $50. Calligraphy sets can be bought at your local office or art supply store. Videotapes and books on calligraphy are available at most large libraries and bookstores. You can teach yourself or take advantage of calligraphy courses offered by local schools.

Once you have a basic grasp of calligraphy, you must continue to practice. It is important to improve both, your quality and efficiency. Speeding up your ability to complete customers' jobs will not only free more time for other work but also increase your rate of pay. If you charge $20 for an invitation and it takes you one hour, you would have gotten an hourly rate of $20 per hour (less supplies). However, if you are able to complete the same invitation in a half hour, you can make an hourly rate of $40 per hour.

EQUIPMENT

A Basic Calligraphy Set
Artist Pad

MARKETING

Getting customers should not be a major hassle. Start locally with your church, shopping centers and the like.
Place fliers detailing your unique skill and talent in local libraries. Call offices and get permission to place your flier
on their bulletin boards. Your flier should state the service
you provide, a telephone number, prices, your name and
the best time to call for an appointment. Your flier should
also be written in calligraphy to give prospective customers
an example of your handiwork.

Send sample letters to business managers/owners, clergy, and associations with an introductory offer to produce a document or invitation for their next event at a reduced rate. Attend local fairs, bazaars and flea markets and set up a booth creating name plates for the attendees.

Get a list of newborns from the city or use your local legal news and write to new parents offering to produce the child's name in calligraphy on a name plate or other such item. This can work at church also, after a baby has been christened. Ask the clergy for permission to post your services in the church bulletin.

As you can see, there are many ways to utilize your new-found skill at a profit. Again, be creative. The more things there are to write about, the more opportunities you have for income. Above all else, you have to be self-motivated and willing to take the time to practice and perfect the art of calligraphy.

PRICING

Review videotapes on calligraphy, use your local **Yellow Pages**, and go to the library to find calligraphy associations to join. These associations will help you improve your skill and guide you in pricing your services. Charges can be based upon the project and the style of writing. Again, local associations will help you with resources and references. A major point to remember in pricing however, is the time it takes to complete the job. Determine how much you want to make hourly. Then, price and complete your work with that in mind.

CAN AND BOTTLE RECYCLING OR RETURN

Many people hate the hassle of returning empty bottles and cans to the store for deposit. The result can be that cans and bottles pile up in homes and businesses or end up in the garbage.

HOW TO GET STARTED

There are many businesses with cafeterias or lunch rooms where employees either bring their own cans and bottles or buy from vending machines. Those cans and bottles tend to pile up. This is where you come in. Go to these businesses and ask if it would be possible for you to provide them with containers for empty cans and bottles. Let them know that you would empty them at whatever schedule you and the customer decide. By leaving a large container for disposal of returnables, you eliminate the need to be there in person, which would be time consuming, impractical and not very profitable. The container will give you the option of having many customers.

Your container should be a standard 40-gallon aluminum or sturdy plastic trash can or one similar with a tight-fitting lid. You will need to label your container with your business' name, making sure it is clear that you are a for-profit com-

pany. It would be wise to make an opening in the top of the container so that cans and bottles can be easily placed but not easily removed by anyone other than yourself. You may want to consider chaining your container to a secure object.

People also tend to let returnables pile up in their homes. This too is an opportunity for you to gain more customers. Elderly, busy and working people would all benefit from having one less chore to do, and you would benefit by providing this service. People may want something for the deposit they paid on the returnables, so offer to come to their homes, collect the returnables and give them half the value of the cans and bottles you collect. For example, if the customer has $5.00 worth of returnables, you would give them

$2.50. You will make the $2.50 back when you return the cans and bottles.

Remember, most people like things to be as easy as possible. You are doing this for them. This idea could apply to apartment buildings, senior citizens' complexes and community centers. The possibilities are plentiful when you think of all the bottles and cans that go unreturned each year.

EQUIPMENT

Containers and Plastic Bags
Chain Lock
Signs on the Containers

MARKETING

There are over two million dollars worth of unreturned cans and bottles each year in Michigan alone. You can create a business from this with hardly any money invested. You simply need the containers for depositing cans and bottles and fliers describing your business.

Keep your fliers simple with important information such as your phone number and details about the service you provide. Make sure you mention that you will provide the container for disposing of the returnables.

CANDY TREES

Candy trees are, by far, one of the easiest and most inexpensive items a person can make. For people looking to give the out-of-the-ordinary, one-of-a-kind gift, candy trees are the perfect answer. If you are a creative and innovative enterpriser, this venture could very well be the start of something big.

HOW TO GET STARTED

All you basically need to make candy trees are fancy glasses or vases, wrapped candy and a large Styrofoam ball. The glasses and vases can be found at discount and dollar stores, garage and estate sales. Wrapped penny or hard candy can be purchased in bulk at wholesalers which can be found in the **Yellow Pages** under "Candy-Wholesale." The Styrofoam balls (3 to 4 inches) and glue gun can be found at an arts and crafts store. You also need fern pins which you can buy at a florist.

Now that you have all the needed materials, begin by filling the glass or vase with anything you want. You can use candy, sea shells, plastic flowers and fruit, colored glass balls, etc. You may want to make your own special design. The possibilities are endless, so it's up to you to be creative.

Using the glue gun, carefully apply glue to the rim of the glass or vase and secure the Styrofoam ball to it. After the

glue dries, lace the ends of the wrapped candy onto the
fern pins. The fern pins should be approximately an inch
long, so it should hold 4
to 6 pieces of average-
size candy. Once this is
done, insert pins into
Styrofoam ball until the
ball is completely cov-
ered.

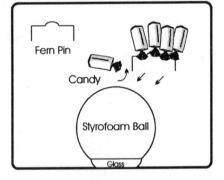

Fern Pin

Candy

Styrofoam Ball

Glass

Here's an idea. Take a
sundae glass and fill it
with wrapped bubble gum. Attach the Styrofoam ball and
cover it with more bubble gum. Place a piece of cherry
candy on the top, cut a piece of a plastic straw and stick it
into the Styrofoam ball, creating a candy tree sundae.

EQUIPMENT

Wrapped Hard or Penny Candy
Styrofoam Balls
Glasses, Mugs or Vases
Glue Gun with Glue
Items to Fill Glasses (Sea Shells, Marbles, Plastic Flowers)

MARKETING

As always, begin with friends and family members. A venture such as this will spread quickly by word of mouth. Your trees are sure to be a hit, especially at Christmas, Mother's and Valentine's Days. It would be a good idea to take pictures and start an album of your creations to have on hand for potential customers to pick from. They may want you to duplicate one, or it could give them an idea of what they want.

As business grows, look into renting a booth at the local flea market on weekends. If business really skyrockets, you may even want to rent a booth at a mall during the Christmas season.

PRICING

Markup your trees at least 200-300%. For example if you spend $5 on supplies, then you want to charge between $15 and $20. Also keep in mind you will want to charge extra for oversized trees and any special requests.

CARWASHING

Getting a car washed at a drive-thru car wash can be easy and inexpensive. But rarely does a car get the good cleaning that a hand carwash service can provide. The automatic cleaning and drying process at drive-thru car washes is rushed, often does not clean hard-to-reach areas and leaves water spots that can lead to rust.

For people who want extra attention and care for their vehicle but simply do not have the time to do it themselves, your at-home hand car wash would be ideal.

HOW TO GET STARTED

Determine how much time it will take to wash an average-sized car inside and out. Then, find out what local hand car washes charge and then set a price that is competitive.

You must decide if you want to offer the option of exterior only or interior and exterior cleaning. It would be a good idea to provide both services and set prices for each to gain more business. If someone only wanted the outside done, you could wash their car right in their driveway and all you would need is the use of their water.

EQUIPMENT & SUPPLIES

Water hose with Nozzle
Soft Cotton Towels, Rags, Chamois (for drying)
Whisk Broom
Cordless Car Vacuum (optional)
Glass Cleaner
Scrub Brush with Soft, Non-Metal Bristles
Dishwashing Liquid
Bucket

MARKETING

The best place to start is with relatives, friends or neighbors
who live near you. Another excellent place to look for business is used car lots. The cars usually remain outside and
look better to potential customers if they are clean. Con-

tracting with used car lots to wash their cars will bring profits to them and you. Passing out fliers door-to-door will
further promote your service. Remember, whatever business you are in you must have a niche. In your flier and
when talking to potential customers, mention the amenities
of your business that are better and more convenient than
your competition. For example:

(1) Customers don't have to leave home.
(2) No tipping required (optional).
(3) Car is completely washed and dried.
(4) Tires are cleaned.
(5) Armorall can be applied (optional).
(6) Soft cloth rags and towels are used.
(7) Air freshener may be provide (optional).

This business offers not only a service but also a convenience for customers. It is hard work but it doesn't take that
much time if you do it right the first time. When you build
up a base of customers whose cars you clean on a regular
basis, the job will be easier and faster. For the most part,
the interior will be clean from the previous washing, so you
may decide only to do the inside once a month or so.

Your job is to do a good, thorough cleaning every time. Be
prompt and professional!

PROFIT - *MEASURING YOUR SUCCESS*

Profit is the difference between a business and a hobby. You must show a profit in order to keep a business going for any length of time.

How To Measure Profit

First figure out how much your goods and/or supplies cost. That can be everything from flour to cleaning solution, rent, helpers and, most importantly, your time. Figure a decent wage for yourself, $10 to $25 per hour. If your business grows, then you should increase the amount of your wage. For every hour you spend working on your business, you should include this amount as an expense. Once you have totaled all costs and expenses, you double or triple this number - keeping in mind that you want to be competitive.

TYPICAL EXPENSE

Cost of Goods (items you sell)   *Overhead* (expense you pay with or without sales)

Cost of Goods	Overhead
Frames	Rent
Glue	Telephone
Glass	Employees
T-Shirts	Advertising
Baskets	Taxes
Pins	Receipts

James Bruce Llewellyn

Opening a retail store in Harlem began the distinguished career of James Llewellyn. While operating this store he attended college and earned several degrees. This was only the beginning. By mortgaging his house and selling all that he owned, Mr. Llewellyn was able to purchase Fedco Foods Corp. This retail business seemed too risky to others who were intimidated by its location on the rough side of town. With many years of hard work, he was able to turn it into the nation's largest minority-owned retail business with annual sales of $100 million.

It wasn't time for him to stop yet. Mr. Llewellyn continues as a force in the business world with numerous ventures, including the purchase of the Philadelphia Coca-Cola Bottling Co., making it the third largest African-American owned business with annual sales of over $290 million.

49

CARPET CLEANING SERVICE

Carpet cleaning involves the use of heavy, cumbersome equipment. Practically every home has carpet that requires cleaning. If you don't mind work that requires some physical exertion, carpet cleaning could be just the ticket. Although start-up costs might be high, you can get used equipment, have your parents rent equipment for you or rent the family's carpet cleaner and vacuum cleaner if available.

HOW TO GET STARTED

Begin by practicing at home or at a relative's house to determine the actual time involved in cleaning. For instance, will it take two hours to clean an average living room with furniture? If the answer is yes, what is the size of the carpet, how much does the competition charge for a similar size room, and do they move the furniture? Now you can determine how much to charge per hour and how much to pay your help. If you pay your help $5 per hour and charge $45 to clean a living room that takes 2 hours to complete, you are $35 ahead, less supply costs. However, if you rent the equipment, you will have to complete at least two or more sales to make a substantial profit.

EQUIPMENT

2 Carpet Cleaners
2 Vacuum Cleaners
2 Packages of Vacuum Cleaning Bags
3 Gallons of Shampoo and Defoaming Agent

MARKETING

Place fliers detailing your unique carpet cleaning services
in the libraries, churches, shopping centers and the like. In
addition, call day care centers. The spills of a small child
can build up and Mom and Dad can be forced to seek a professional. Marketing your service to the parents of children
at day care centers could be a great niche. The flier should
state the service you provide, a telephone number, prices,
your name and the best time to call for an appointment.

To make your service more marketable, add a unique feature to your package. For instance, offer monthly carpet spot and stain control maintenance for $5 to $10 a month. Think how much money you can make after school if you have several customers in an apartment complex.

BUSINESS TIP

ADVERTISING

The way to inform people about your business is through advertising. In order to get customers, they must know you exist. There are many ways to go about this.

Fliers are usually inexpensive and direct. If you do not mind a little foot work, you can save yourself some money. Copy centers, like **Kinkos**, have on-site desktop publishing for developing fliers and brochures. You can either rent time on a computer and develop your own flier or pay to have a staff person develop one for you. Small neighborhood newspapers are sometimes reasonable if you have a small ad. Make sure the people you want to reach are going to read this paper. You do not want to advertise Christmas items in an Islamic newspaper, for example. Most newspapers can provide demographics or literature with information on how many people read it and what their interest are.

COMPUTER CONSULTING

A lmost everyone has a computer today, however very few people use their computer to its fullest potential. As a young person, you probably have some knowledge of computers without the fear of them that a great number of adults have. If you have a computer or access to one, selling your expertise can become a money-making venture for you.

HOW TO GET STARTED

You will first need to determine the most common uses for home computers, for example word processing, financial record-keeping and database creation. Talk to family and friends who have home computers to find out what areas they are having trouble with and to establish what services you will need to perform. Once you have established what services home computer owners need most, simply direct your advertising and your business toward their needs. It is important that you know how to perform all of these services before you get your customers.

You should also become familiar with the most commonly-used software. Because many people find computers confusing, it would be beneficial to you to determine the most common questions people have about their home computers in order to add to your expertise.

There may be functions your customer's computer can perform that they do not know exist. If you find ways for your customer to maximize their computer usage, you will be doing them a great service. For example, speeding up the computer's performance, cleaning up the computer's directories, installing anti-virus software and showing how to access free software are all benefits you could provide to your customer. You may also want to offer training that will enable them to perform some tasks without your assistance.

MARKETING

Starting out with friends and family is a great beginning. However, you can expand your business by advertising. A few good places to start are churches, computer store bulletin boards as well as bulletin boards in apartment buildings and grocery stores. You will need to develop a professional flier listing the services you provide, pricing and most importantly where and when you can be reached. It is also a good idea to make your flier on your computer and use eye-catching graphics to make it stand out. There's nothing wrong with showing off your abilities a little because the first impression is the most important one!

Also offer a debugging service. People are becoming more concerned with viruses showing up in their system. These viruses can slow down the system's performance and even cause loss of files and information. There are many inexpensive software programs available to debug and protect your client's computer from current and future viruses. Try to use public domain software, which are computer programs available to the general public and can be used and duplicated at no charge. If you use private or published software, be sure not to duplicate it.

PRICING

As a computer consultant, you are selling your knowledge and your time. Check the **Yellow Pages** as well as local newspapers to determine how much computer consultants are charging in your area. This will give you an idea of what to charge for your services.

CUSTOM FRAMING

Custom framing is an emerging service within the African-American community and it is growing like wildfire. For a young person who is good with their hands and understands math, this could be a business that easily blossoms into a career. This service is recommended for older teens because it deals with glass and sharp tools.

WHAT YOU NEED TO GET STARTED

There are five basic steps to custom framing. Decide what type of frames you think are popular. Initially, you may want to carry five to ten types of the most popular frames.

The Frames

You can find out what types of frames are popular by calling frame wholesalers and asking for the top ten metal and wood frames. As a rule, #5 gold, silver and black will be your biggest sellers no matter who you buy from (#5 is a style of aluminum frame). When buying aluminum frames always ask if they come in a generic version. Wood frames are going to be a little tougher to judge. There are no standards, so take a trip out to one of the wholesalers to see what type of frames you want to offer. You can usually buy corner samples of the frames that interest you. You can find these places by looking in the phone book under "Picture Frames -Wholesale."

The Glass

Glass is sold by glass wholesalers and some frame whole-salers. However, glass and frame wholesalers sell only in large quantities. One way around this is to buy single strength window glass straight from the hardware store. The glass will cost a little more, but you have the conven-ience of having it cut to the size you want.

Mounting

Mounting is the process of laying and attaching a docu-ment, photo or poster to a board so that it will lay flat un-der glass when it is in a frame. You have two choices when it comes to deciding what boards to use. One choice is regular poster or mounting board. This is the least ex-pensive but the board is really flimsy and usually requires a second sheet made of corrugated cardboard to make the poster board more sturdy. The second choice would be foam board, which is white board roughly 1/4 inch thick. It has a smooth surface that is great for mounting and a thick, rigid center that does not require any additional back-ing. Foam board is definitely the preferred choice. Both come in standard sizes and can be bought in single sheets at frame wholesalers or art supply stores.

(1) The easiest form of attachment is a standard hinge mount, which is done by placing removable drafting tape across the top of the document to secure it in place.

(2) Spray Mount is the use of spray adhesive (one popular brand is Photo Mount) which is simply sprayed on the board according to the instructions. Make sure you are in

a well-ventilated area and are not exposed to flames from a furnace or water heater. Also, give yourself ample room when working with spray adhesive -- it gets on everything. Spray adhesive works well on small documents and photos under 16 x 20 inches.

(3) Drymounting and vacuum mounting are the most so-phisticated ways to mount posters and prints. These two processes require a press which costs between $700 and $3,500 each depending on the size. The process of dry-mounting takes all the wrinkles out of any poster or docu-ment and mounts it to the foamboard or mounting board -- permanently! Explain this to your customers before agree-ing to do this. Drymounting is the best treatment for post-ers and prints larger than 16 x 20 inches. If your customer is giving you a collectible or rare item, do not dry or spray mount the item, it will decrease the its value. Most kids

and adults cannot afford a press in the beginning, so it would be smart to cut a deal with a local frame shop that has a press to do your drymounting until you purchase your own.

Matting

Matting is the addition of color boards around the perimeter of a picture or document. This process involves selecting coordinating colors then cutting an opening in the board to allow the picture to show through. Mats also come in samples that you can buy from a frame wholesaler.

MARKETING

Keep in mind special occasions and holidays for marketing your service. One ideal way to drum up business is by offering special discounts to those who may get pictures framed often, such as lawyers, doctors and other businesspeople. There are plenty of ways to promote framing. The Professional Picture Framers Association is a great group to join for assistance in your venture. Write them at 4305 Sarellen Rd., Richmond, VA 23231. Or call them at (800) 832-7732.

PRICING

Once you have decided what type of framing you will provide, determine what the frame job is going to cost you. When you have your cost of goods, mark up the amount so that it is profitable, usually 200 percent. If your cost is $10, for example, then you should charge around $30. Framing is a time-consuming business, so allow yourself enough time to complete your projects safely and with quality.

Warren E. Anderson

What kid hasn't squealed with delight at the toy inside the Happy Meal? A lot of those toys come from The Anderson-DuBose Company, as well as the hamburgers, fish and chicken patties, lettuce, tomatoes and dairy products.

Who's responsible? Warren E. Anderson, president of The Anderson-DuBose Company, which is one of 40 McDonald's distributors and the sixth largest African-American company in the U.S. with sales in 1993 of $115 million.

Mr. Anderson began his career in broadcasting where he held various positions in radio and television. Determination and perseverance paid off in 1991 when he and Steve DuBose purchased 51 percent of The Martin-Bower Company to become the first and only minority distributor in the McDonald's distribution network.

ETHNIC CHRISTMAS ORNAMENTS

Decorating the Christmas tree is a timeless tradition and people are becoming more creative and symbolic with the types of ornaments they put on their trees. This is the perfect opportunity for someone to offer ornaments that are both beautiful and meaningful.

HOW TO GET STARTED

First, select fabric that you are going to use. Next, cut 10 inch circles, roughly the size of a small dinner plate, out of fabric for each ornament. Using a 2 to 3 inch Styrofoam ball, the fabric should be large enough to cover the entire ball and have excess material at the top of the ball. Simply wrap the Styrofoam ball with the fabric and tie a rubber band around the top of the material. A screw hook is then inserted and glued into the ball at the top where the rubber band is. This will hold the gold or silver elastic string which hangs the balls on the tree limbs. Use a gold pipe cleaner to cover the rubber band, wrapping it around several times. In no time you have beautiful Christmas ornaments. You can make even more elaborate ornaments by adding glitter and/or sequins to them. They can be sold in sets of the same or mixed patterns.

EQUIPMENT

Styrofoam Balls and Screw Hooks
African Pattern Material
Gold or Silver, Elastic String, Pipe Cleaner, Glitter, and Sequins
Scissors and Rubber Bands

MARKETING

Because this business is seasonal, the best time to begin
would be as early as possible. Some people put up their
Christmas trees as early as Thanksgiving, so it would be ad-
vantageous for you to have your product ready for sale by
the beginning of November. Your teachers, friends and
family would be a good place to start. You may also consider setting up in front of banks, grocery stores and other
businesses. Your church is another very good place for

such a venture. The local church probably puts up a Christmas tree and this would be a wonderful advertisement for your product. Since this is a holiday item, you want to get as much exposure as possible in a short period of time. Ask friends and family members if they would be willing to place a little Christmas tree on their desks at work decorated with your ornaments. This would give you a lot of exposure, and the opportunity to take orders for your product. Don't limit your product to just your own ethnic group. With a little research, you could make these ornaments with traditional colors and patterns from many different ethnic groups.

IDENTIFICATION

It is almost impossible to do business without some type of formal identification. You are now in business so you will need to open a checking and/or savings account. You may also need to rent equipment or cash a customer's check, which requires formal identification.

If you are 16 you may already have your driver's license, which is considered adequate identification at most banks. However, if you don't have your license at 16, or are under the age of 16, you still need identification. In this case you would go to the same institution that handles driver's licenses and apply for a state identification card. Another piece of ID to always have on hand is your social security card.

GENERAL MERCHANDISING

General merchandising is a very broad and wide open field. Basically, you have the benefit of selling just about anything. Kmart, Sears and Walmart are considered general merchandisers. They sell everything from deodorant to lawn mowers. Of course, it is unreasonable to think you have the money to stock all these different items. But if you understand the principle of buying wholesale and selling retail, whenever you consider carrying a product you will know what to do.

WHAT TO SELL

If you know that a family or class reunion is coming up and the organizers will need to buy large quantities of t-shirts, mugs, glasses, hats or pens, there is no reason why you could not offer one or more of these items at a competitive price. You may consider approaching local softball and bowling leagues, as well. The key is knowing how to get the product.

HOW TO BUY MERCHANDISE WHOLESALE

First, know your product. You do not want to get your merchandise from the same places your customers can. To find "real" wholesalers you will have to spend some time in the business department of the library. A great source for suppliers is the **Yellow Pages Business-to-Business** direc-

tory. If you live in a small city or community, you may want to look at a larger city's **Yellow Pages**, such as those in Chicago, New York or Los Angeles. Just make sure you are dealing with wholesalers or manufacturers.

Another great source for finding wholesalers is the **Thomas Register**, an encyclopedia of wholesalers and manufacturers around the country. If your product is mass produced, you may look at getting it from another country. A great deal of products sold in the U.S.A. are made overseas. There are **Yellow Pages** for countries like Taiwan, China, Hong Kong, Singapore and Mexico. It may be impractical to buy from these companies direct, but usually they have contacts established in the U.S. that will sell to you directly. All these books are available at most libraries.

DEALING WITH OUT-OF-TOWN COMPANIES

If you contact out-of-state suppliers, don't worry. In most cases they will ship a product and you pay upon receipt of the merchandise.

Some suppliers will ask for a deposit. This is not uncommon if you are ordering large quantities or custom-made products. If you are uncomfortable with giving a deposit, you may want to contact the Better Business Bureau in your city and get information on how long a particular company has been in business and if there are any complaints on their record.

After contacting a reputable supplier who has given you the best price, you must find out how long it will take to get the merchandise, especially if you need it for an event or by a specific date.

There are several occasions when people buy merchandise in large quantities. For example:

Weddings
Birthday Parties
Family Reunions
Graduations
High School Senior Trips
Political Functions
Church Functions

HOLIDAY CARD SELLING

Nearly everyone buys greeting cards. It is a tradition in this country that will probably never end. As long as that is true, you can grow a business from it. There are many kinds of cards for all types of occasions. However, holiday cards are probably where you can make the most money. Christmas, Father's Day and Mother's Day are the biggest sellers of the year. So why not get in on this business?

HOW TO GET STARTED

The equipment you will need to start this business is simple: the cards themselves. The best place to buy cards would be through manufacturers or wholesalers. Broom Design, located at 16180 Meyers Ave., Detroit, MI 48235 or call at (313) 863-6158 and Things Graphics, located at 1522 14th St., N.W., Washington, D.C. 20005 or call at (202) 667-4028 are two companies that produce ethnic greeting cards. However, if there are other cards you like and think would sell, just look on the back of the card for the name of the manufacturer.

MARKETING

It is best to begin with family and friends. Have your parents take samples with them to work. Because of the nature of this business, visibility is your best friend. A major selling point is that customers would not have to fight the crowds at card shops. They choose from your samples and the cards are delivered directly to them. Also, find a place where you may be able to sell your cards temporarily such as grocery stores, florists or neighborhood banks. Getting permission shouldn't be a problem since you would not be in direct competition with these businesses. If you are going to set up outside a business, make sure your display table is neat and professional and that you are as well. Be polite and courteous, but also be vocal. People will treat you like a bump on a log if you act like one. Most importantly, you must have enough of your products to sell.

BUYING OVERSEAS

Finding an overseas supplier is as easy
as going to your local library. Refer to
the business section of the library where
you will find the **Business Yellow**
Pages from all parts of the world. Most companies that ad-
vertise in these books are looking to do business with companies in the U.S. When looking at the **Business Yellow**
Pages of a particular country, write down a few different
suppliers to ensure that you have several different sources
for goods and prices. Keep in mind that in order to contact
these companies, you may have to call the telephone opera-
tor to get the country code. In addition, be aware of the
time difference between your U.S. region and the country
you're calling. Most businesses operate from 9 a.m. to 5
p.m. just like the U.S. However, the key is to know when
it is 9 a.m. in the country you are calling.

Once you reach a supplier, you may be greeted with a non-
English speaking employee. Don't worry, these companies want to do business with the U. S. and will usually
have at least one employee that speaks English. The best
approach without confusing the person on the phone is to
simply say the word "English." It would be even more
helpful if you learned to say "who speaks English?" in the
language of the country you are calling. Once you have a
person that can communicate with you, approach them the
same way you would a local supplier. Often large foreign
manufacturers can't supply you if your quantities are too
small, but they may have relatives or associates in the U.S.
that can, with only a slight increase in price.

LANDSCAPING

L awn mowing is a service widely used by adults during spring and summer months. There are plenty of opportunities to gain clients in this area and they are usually not far from home. Because it is usually one of their chores, many young people have a certain amount of lawn mowing experience. They have also learned the most efficient ways to get the job done so they can move on to other things. But, if you are smart, you can turn this experience into a money-making venture.

HOW TO GET STARTED

It would be a good idea to have a daily planner to schedule all your jobs and personal responsibilities. The landscaping business can be easy to manage since most jobs occur weekly or biweekly on the same day, usually at the same time. It is important to give yourself enough time between jobs. If you have a problem making it to a job, contact the customer as soon as possible. Most people will be understanding if you give them early notice, but make it a point to get there later the same day or at the very latest, the next morning. People who pay to have their lawns maintained usually are very proud of how it looks and do not enjoy letting it go undone.

EQUIPMENT & SUPPLIES

Lawn Mower
Rake
Lawn Edger (optional)
Hedge Clipper (optional)
Bags for Clippings

Purchasing a brand new lawn mower can be quite expensive for a young businessperson. People are always buying new lawn mowers in the spring and usually sell or trade in their old ones. A good place to look for a good used lawn mower is in the classifieds of your local newspaper, lawn mower retailers and especially lawn mower service repair shops. Repair shops may be able to offer you the best deal. Often times, a person will take their lawn mower in for repair and never pick it up. In this case, you may be able to get a good running mower for the cost of repairs.

When you find a mower, make sure it runs well. This means being able to start repeatedly without hesitation. It is a waste of time and money to buy a lawn mower at a steal if it doesn't work. Remember, you are going into the landscaping business, not lawn mower repair!

Other supplies should be rather easy to come by.

MARKETING

Family members can be your first chance to establish a customer base. For the enterprising young person, a flier passed door-to-door could further establish your business. This flier must be well done and professional because it

will be the first impression of your business. The flier (see sample on page 53), should include your name, phone number, what services you provide and, if possible, your rate. (Note: pay attention to the lawns where you leave fliers. If the yard requires more-than-average work, do not leave an average quote.)

PRICING

Landscaping is a service business; you are selling labor. You must price your work based on how long it will take you. If a job takes an hour, then you must decide how much one hour of your time is worth. Typically, you wouldn't want to ask less than $10.00 an hour for landscaping or any labor-related job. Once you are in business, you can roll the labor price into one quote. For example, if you were to charge $15.00 for a job, this price would include your $10.00 per hour for labor plus $5.00 for supplies and travel. Probably the best way to find pricing information is to call your competitors. Look in the **Yellow Pages** under "landscaping,"and call a couple of different businesses and ask them for a quote on your parents' lawn (get your parents' permission first). They may be able to quote you a price over the phone. Once you have this information, you will have a better idea of how to set your own prices.

Most customers will not put too many demands on you especially if you list exactly what you will do on your flier. Discussing with your potential customer any additional services will help you to adjust your pricing and eliminate having to raise your price later. Another good way to avoid any misunderstandings is to offer additional services and their cost. You could simply list these on your flier.

For example:

Planting Flowers
Fertilizing
Rotill Garden
Trimming Studs
Weeding Garden
Spraying Weeds

Sharon L. McWhorter

When Sharon Louise McWhorter was seven years old, Santa Claus asked what she wanted for Christmas. Her reply was "a bag full of money." Sharon McWhorter has continued to pursue that goal.

At the age of 26, she started her first corporation to market her invention, a nationally distributed cup-holder for bicycles. Four years later, she formed SMJ Corridor Development Company, a partnership that bought an historic school building, and converted it into an office building that provides support services for other entrepreneurs. At the age of 32, she launched American Resource Training System, Inc. to provide entrepreneurial, corporate, management and personnel development training to major corporations nationally. At the age of 36 she was profiled in **The Marquis Who's Who of American Women**.

LETTERING T-SHIRTS & HATS

Most every group or organization has hats and T-shirts depicting their name, logo or slogan. Custom lettering on hats or T-shirts could be a good business for the young person who has both the time and desire to go out and get the business.

HOW TO GET STARTED

First, decide if you are going to use pre-cut letters or custom letters you cut out of fabric. Pre-cut letters have adhesive on the back and are ready to apply. If your project requires an extra flair, you may cut letters out of the fabric of your choice. To attach your custom cut letters, use a fabric adhesive, such as Wonder Under. This is a thin sheet of adhesive, similar to wax paper, that is cut to the shape of each letter. The fabric adhesive is placed between the letter and the shirt or hat. When a hot iron is applied to letters, the fabric adhesive melts and permanently attaches the letter to the garment. Both pre-cut letters and fabric adhesive, along with additional instructions, are available at your local arts and crafts store. To find T-shirt and hat suppliers, look in the **Yellow Pages** under T-Shirts -Wholesale or use the **Business-to-Business** version, which can be found at your local library.

Keep in mind that if you are starting a business in which you don't have a lot of experience, it is always wise to practice before seeking customers. Never practice on customers! It's bad for business and your reputation as a competent business person. Be creative with your lettering. Use different letter styles and various colors. People like to be different, so use this to your advantage.

EQUIPMENT

Fabric (various colors and prints)
Pre-cut Lettering
Iron and Iron Adhesive (adheres fabric to hat or T-shirt)
T-Shirts and Hats

MARKETING

When working with personalized items, it is best to start where people use these types of items--such as churches, social clubs, civic and community organizations, schools, fraternities and sororities. Some companies sponsor sports teams that would need personalized hats and/or T-shirts. Contact with these types of organizations could begin with members. Or if you don't know anyone, send letters to the organizations directly. Try to meet with whoever is in charge. You would then have the opportunity to show samples of your professionally-done T-shirts and hats.

BUSINESS TIP

RESOURCES: How to find wholesalers
No matter what business you are interested in, you will need suppliers. First identify what your product or service is, then figure what industry it falls into.
Once this is determined, you can find your own suppliers.

Your local library business section is a great place to start. Key places to look for suppliers are the **Business Yellow Pages**, **Thomas Register** and trade magazines for your particular industry. Also, if you are interested in buying a product made by a particular manufacturer but cannot find the phone number or address, for a charge of 75 cents, you can call (900)GET-INFO. They will provide you with the phone number of any listed company within the U.S. without knowing their exact location. Be sure to get your parents permission before using this number.

MICROWAVE COOKING COOKBOOK FOR KIDS

There are several microwave cookbooks on the market today. However, how many cookbooks do you think were designed specifically for kids using the microwave? Not many, if any. Your creation would be a great addition to an underdeveloped market. Most kids and their parents use the microwave to reheat pizza, leftovers and restaurant take-outs. Think about the foods you and your friends like to eat and how you can use your microwave to not only cook some of these foods, but perhaps create some new taste sensations.

HOW TO GET STARTED

Today there are several cooking shows and videos on microwave cooking. Rent a videotape from the library or take a look at the cookbook that came with your microwave and start from there. Of course, you will want to get your parent's permission to use the kitchen, but I am sure they won't mind if it means you will be doing some of the cooking. Review your favorite kids' and grown-ups' recipes, and select the ones you, your friends and family like the most. Experiment with the ingredients and test their eye and taste appeal. Change the recipes to suit your tastes and use a computer to write your book.

Writing a cookbook isn't easy, but it's not impossible. It is primarily discipline and an eagerness to express yourself with words. Start-up costs are really quite low. All you

need is a library card or time to watch cooking shows on
television, some food and willing taste testers. Initially,
everything you need is probably already in your kitchen.
Once you are ready to develop the actual book, make sure
that it uses the same format as other cookbooks, by showing
ingredients and order of preparation.

Printing a book can also be very expensive. One way to
keep this cost down, is to have a copy center, like **Kinkos**,
photocopy and bind copies of the book as you need them. If
your book is under 50 pages, you can use clear report hold-
ers, which can bought at your local office supply store. Always check around for the best price.

Don't forget to copyright your book to protect your rights.
The library offers books and videos on the copyright process, which is not difficult.

EQUIPMENT

Microwave and Manufacturer's Cookbook
Glass Cooking Dishes
Measuring Cups and Spoons
Plastic Storage Containers
Wax Paper and Aluminum Foil
Recipe File Holder and Blank Index Cards
Computer and Printer (optional)

MARKETING

Offer to do cooking demonstrations at local bookstores, supermarkets, chain stores, church fairs and the like. Have
your book available for purchase. You can also use the
book as a product to sell for church fundraisers. Run classified ads in children's and parenting magazines. Get free
publicity by sending a press release to local newspapers, radio programs and television stations. Again, the library is a
prime source on how to do press releases.

Write to the various microwave manufacturers telling them
about your new book and the fact that it is written for kids
by a young adult. Ask them to include it in their product
packaging. You will fill the orders, sharing a small percentage of sales with the manufacturer.

PRICING

Determine your printing costs. Then compare the prices for
children's cookbooks and the number of recipes and pictures to microwave cookbooks in general. You want to
make sure that your selling price is at least double your
printing cost.

BUSINESS PLAN

Making a business plan is a very
important part of a business. A
business plan is as important to a
business as a road map is to a
truck driver. Simply put, a business plan is a written list of some
of the important parts of your

business. You want to write it as if you were explaining
your business to a total stranger.

Answer a few questions:

What service or product am I selling?
Who do I want to sell to?
What makes my product or service better?
How much does my product or service cost me?
How much does it sell for and is my price competitive?
How am I going to get my customers?
*What are the things I am going to need to start my business and how
much is it going to cost?*
What do I expect to have in one year - sales, profits, customers etc.?

Constructing a one-year plan would be a good start. Most
business plans are written to include from 5 to more than 100
years depending on the size of the company. Just keep your
goals within reason. The plan itself is a great source of refer-
ence to make sure that you are on the right track. Also, writing a business plan helps you answer some very important
questions that you may otherwise overlook regarding your
business.

Costello Johnson

When you walk into an office you may not notice the furniture. Not because it's unattractive, but because you know it's supposed to be there. Things that we take for granted are making millions of dollars for someone. In the case of office furniture, that someone is Costello Johnson, owner of Corporate Office Systems. Mr. Johnson had held various positions in the office furniture industry before starting C.O.S., which in the last five years has become a $16 million a year company. From his position on various boards to his ownership of C.O.S., Mr. Johnson has proven that there are opportunities all around.

PAINTED & AIRBRUSHED T-SHIRTS

T-shirts are always in style and are worn by children and adults alike. The key to making this venture a success is to use your imagination to make your shirts as creative as possible. Many people get T-shirts made to announce an event, such as a family reunion, but many more buy them because of a catchy slogan or an attractive design. The key is to find popular images and identify a customer who would buy them if painted on a T-shirt. You can use anything from Nefertiti dressed in kente cloth to a picture of the your city's skyline. Seasonal, holiday and personalized T-shirts make this business open to endless opportunities.

HOW TO GET STARTED

This business requires some imagination and artistic ability since you will be painting directly onto a T-shirt. There will be times, however, when a more detailed design is required and you don't want to risk freehand painting. When this occurs, you should use transfers sheets (sheets which can be painted on and then transferred onto T-shirts) so if you make a mistake, you waste a transfer sheet rather than a T-shirt. Transfer sheets can be purchased at any arts and crafts store. When creating your image, regular fabric paint is the least expensive route. All you need is a variety of paint colors and standard artist brushes in a variety of sizes. Although airbrushing is more costly, it is becoming

the technique of choice for a lot of new artist and designers. Airbrushing is the process by which paint is sprayed and controlled through a tool called a "gun." This gun holds a small amount of paint which is dispersed by the air produced by an aerosol can or compressor. With proper training and practice, an airbrush may offer an additional flair to your creation. The cost of airbrush systems can range between $100 to $1,000, so shop around.

When creating your image, you could give the design a little extra punch by adding rhinestones, studs, glitter and the like. However, you will want to give your customer instructions on how to wash this particular garment by hand. Also, don't limit yourself to standard T-shirts. Today, women are wearing shoulder padded, oversized T-shirts along with matching stretch pants. These outfits have an unique design on the T-shirt which can also appear on the pants. When shopping for garments, you want to get the best price possible. You also want your product to last, so don't compromise the quality of your shirts and pants. T-shirts can be purchased from wholesalers or on sale at department stores. You may use the **Yellow Pages** or **Business-to-Yellow Pages** to contact wholesalers. Always call more than one to get the best price.

All your painting equipment can be purchased from arts and crafts stores. A salesperson will usually be able to tell you how to use the paints and explain the use of transfers. Don't be afraid to ask sales people for suggestions and advice.

EQUIPMENT

Paint Brushes
Acrylic Paint
Tulip Paint (glitter, puff, slick)
Transfer Paper and Pen
Iron
T-shirts in Various Sizes and Colors (if desired)

MARKETING

Use your imagination. Your creations as well as holiday and personalized designs will allow you to attract more customers. Bazaars and flea markets may serve as a good source for customers. With unique creations, it is important for individuals to wear your goods to show them off. This form of word-of-mouth advertising should prove successful if you are producing attractive and good quality T-shirts and outfits.

PAINTING & GENERAL REPAIR

As long as walls are made of drywall and plaster, they will require painting and plastering. If you have some painting experience, don't mind a little physical labor and have a good eye for color, painting can provide reasonable income with minimal investment.

HOW TO GET STARTED

Painting is not a very complicated process, however it is important to prepare your job site and walls carefully to avoid costly mistakes. Learn to identify which walls will need priming (applying inexpensive white paint first to cut down on the number of coats needed of more expensive paint). For example, all new drywall requires priming as do all new plaster repairs and walls previously painted dark colors that are now going to be painted a light color. Talking to painting professionals or your local paint supplier will help you determine how to approach your job site and customers. Don't forget the library offers books and videos on house painting. You may also have to do some spackling and caulking--used to fill cracks and holes in walls--so it is important that you are knowledgeable about these techniques.

EQUIPMENT & SUPPLIES

Many of the things you will need for this venture are probably in your garage or basement. If you must make purchases, first try garage sales or the classified ads under "Misc. for sale." Equipment can also be bought very reasonably at your local hardware or paint supply store. It's not a bad idea to establish a relationship with one store to buy your supplies. As you become a regular customer, you can look forward to volume discounts and/or good customer discounts for your valued business.

Quality Paint, Paint Brushes and Scrapers
Step and Extension Ladders
Joint Compound, Drop Cloths and Paint Thinner
Quality Rollers, Roller Covers and Extension Handles
Electric or Manual Sander with Sandpaper

MARKETING

Most of your sales and marketing can be done through fliers posted at libraries, supermarkets and local churches, or in local block club newsletters and newspaper classified sections. In addition, many colleges and universities have local newsletters where you can place your ads. Remember to list the best time to call and some of your prices.

Try to offer a bonus of some sort to promote the use of your services, such as a 25 percent reduction on all priming, with a four-room paint order. Another idea would be to get painters' caps and T-shirts with your company name on them. Leave some with your customers that place large paint orders. Be creative!

PRICING

First, compare your prices with your competitor's. You can do this by reviewing the classified section, often under the heading of "Services" or something similar. Determine what the going rate is for a standard room and the number of coats of paint applied. The can of paint will tell you the total wall coverage in square feet. While comparison shopping, it would also be smart to find out the best and most common brand of paint being used by professionals. You don't want to buy a cheap brand that may require applying 3 or 4 coats. Investing a few more dollars on a good quality paint will most likely prove to be more profitable when looking at the extra time and paint. You can practice by painting your own room. Time yourself. How long did it take you? How many coats of paint? Did the coverage match the manufacturer's claim? You will want to charge separately for painting windows sashes, door frames, and wall moldings. These items are referred to as "trimming." Remember to bill separately for trimming since it will require more precision and time.

SAFETY

Whenever you use equipment and supplies or interact with the public, make sure you do it in a safe manner. If you purchase anything from a lawn mower to  a needle and some thread, be sure to read instructions thoroughly. It is also important to have either an expert or parent familiar with the equipment train you on the proper use of it.

When working on a specific task, especially when using equipment, make sure to allow yourself plenty of time to complete it. A great number of accidents are caused by rushing.

If you are dealing with the public, it is very important to have a responsible guardian assist you. You should never enter a stranger's house. There are a lot of people who will harm or take advantage of children.

Geralda L. Dodd

Y ou've often heard about starting at the bottom and working your way up, but does that really happen? If you asked Geralda Dodd, the answer would be a resounding yes!

Ms. Dodd began her career in the steel industry as a receptionist. Navigating her way through the ranks, she was eventually named vice president. In 1990, armed with experience and the dream to own her own steel company, Ms. Dodd and a partner purchased NPS Metals Service, renaming it Integrated Steel Inc. ISI supplies steel products to vendors from both the agricultural and automotive industries who in turn supply Chrysler, General Motors and other major corporations. She also purchased HS Automotive, a supplier of stamped steel parts. Gross sales of both companies for 1993 were an estimated $40 million.

PERSONALIZED GIFT BASKETS

People sometimes have difficulty finding the right gift for birthdays, Father's or Mother's days, Valentine's Day, Secretary's Day or even going-away presents. Personalized gift baskets are the perfect answer for the person who has everything. The best part of this business is the person buying the basket can be sure that the person receiving it will love it. The possibilities are endless.

HOW TO GET STARTED

"Personalized" is the key. Most gift baskets usually contain cheese and fruit. But this basket should be designed especially for the person receiving it. If someone likes golfing for example, you would design a golfing gift basket filled with balls, tees, gloves, etc. If the person is into knitting, you would create a basket full of things related to knitting, such as crocheting needles, yarn, patterns, etc. All the customer needs to do is tell you what the person likes and the rest is up to you. Be as creative and elaborate as possible.

To assemble baskets, fill the bottom of the basket with a bed of color tissue or colored plastic grass (commonly used in Easter baskets). Next, decoratively arrange gift items on bedding. Place basket on top of large sheet of colored acetate. Finally, bring ends of acetate to the top of the basket and tie with ribbon.

Most items can be found at a local arts and crafts store. Give yourself plenty of time to put the baskets together, so you can deliver the product when you said you would. It would be detrimental for you and your customer to be late for someone's special occasion.

EQUIPMENT

Straw Baskets (various sizes)
Colored Acetate or Cellophane for Wrapping
Colored Tissue for Bedding
Ribbon and Small Gift Cards

MARKETING

The actual work involved in making these baskets is minimal. Your imagination will be your greatest asset. It is a good idea to make samples of your work and have your parents take them to work for potential customers to see. You may also consider renting a booth at a local flea market or mall to sell your items.

Of course you will want to make your fliers creative and suggestive. Many people are tired of buying shirts and blouses for their friends and family. They are looking for something unique. Mention this in your flier. Place your fliers in places where there is a lot of activity and movement such as hospitals and universities. These places usually have bulletin boards for such postings. When you receive those calls, as you surely will, be professional and offer to show samples of your work. The quality and creativity of your work will insure a continuous flow of new and repeat customers.

BUSINESS TIP

SEEKING MENTORS

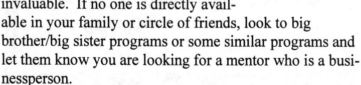

People who are knowledgeable in business prove to be great sources for tips and advice. Seek out that uncle, aunt, family friend or other relative that runs their own business. Their input can be invaluable. If no one is directly available in your family or circle of friends, look to big brother/big sister programs or some similar programs and let them know you are looking for a mentor who is a businessperson.

REALTY HOUSE CLEANING

Don't panic! This isn't your typical house cleaning business. Your customers are real estate companies looking to have homes cleaned before the buyers move in. Believe it or not, a lot of companies look for individuals or companies to clean residential property after the contractors have finished their jobs, but prior to new owner occupancy.

HOW TO GET STARTED

This business does not require much technical skill or supplies. You bill for both your labor and materials. Quite often you can use your parents' vacuum cleaner, mop, broom and buckets until you can afford your own. Reliable transportation is a must.

EQUIPMENT

Detergent
Mop & Buckets
Vacuum Cleaners & Bags
Heavy Duty Extension Cords

Broom & Dust Pan
Rubber Gloves
Tile & Bath Cleansers

MARKETING

Consult your local **Yellow Pages** and contact various real estate agencies. Ask for the manager or owner and tell them about your cleaning service. Prepare fliers and a price list and mail them to prospective Realtors and follow up with a phone call. A great idea to make your business even more impressive would be to leave your own special calling card, such as flowers, balloons or a box of candy, for the new home owners. This will certainly catch the eye of the new home owners who will compliment the realty company and they in turn will probably send more business your way.

PRICING

Most cleaning companies base their prices on the size of
the house or the number of rooms. However, you should
have a minimum price, such as $45 per house. Time your-
self on cleaning an empty house if possible. You don't
want to earn less than $10/hr. in the event you have to hire
someone at $5/hr. or split the job. Additionally, you want
to price windows separately from the entire job.

When you bill your customer, separate your supply costs
from your labor. For example, the total bill is $45 of which
$25 is labor and $20 are supplies. This breakdown will pre-
vent taxes being withheld on the entire amount as labor.
Some Realtors withhold taxes on your earnings, but this is
applicable only to the actual labor portion of your bill.

BUSINESS TIP

WISH LIST

Christmas and Birthdays are the
perfect time to build up your
business needs.
When you are expecting pre-
sents for a birthday or other holidays, instead of asking for
typical gifts like video cartridges or expensive gym shoes,
ask for that edger you need for your landscaping business
or for some extra baskets for your personalized gift basket
business. This is a perfect way to test your own discipline,
dedication and commitment to your business.

SELLING AUTOGRAPHED BOOKS & PICTURES

Celebrity autographs have always been popular. Whether actors, singers or politicians, people love to have their autographs. Starting a service that provides autographed photographs would be unique and profitable.

HOW TO GET STARTED

The most obvious way to get an autograph is to ask for it. Start with the celebrities in your hometown such as sports figures, the mayor, singers or performers. Or try going to concerts, plays and sporting events where celebrities may be. Have your photos or program books ready and simply ask for the person's autograph.

If this is not possible, address books with famous names will be a perfect tool to get the photos and autographs. **The Address Book** *by Micheal Levine* and **The African American Address Book** *by Tabatha Crayton* are books that list the addresses of most famous people. These books contain addresses of all types of celebrities. Simply write to the address listed in the book and ask for an autographed photo. Remember to include a stamped, self-addressed envelope to get better results because there is no cost to the celebrity.

In addition, you can usually get autographed photos through the talent agency that handles them.

Autograph Pricing Guide - this book will tell you the going price for famous autographs. Of course the most expensive autographs will come from celebrities who are dead or unwilling to sign autographs. But, just because a celebrity's autograph price is low doesn't mean everyone has it. It just means they are more willing to sign autographs. And the people you will be selling to will most likely not have their autograph anyway.

SUPPLIES

Self-Addressed Stamped Envelopes 10" X 12"
Sheets of 8 1/2" X 11" Cardboard for Securing Photos

MARKETING

Family and friends are great potential customers for your service. Find out their favorite stars or athletes and start your search. Having specific photos and autographs in mind will save you a lot of time and especially money by not stocking up on autographs that are not selling.

Also, leave your business card or flier at baseball card stores, comic book stores and other rare, collectible retailers. These places are frequented by people who'd be interested in your product or service.

BUSINESS TIP

BUSINESS CARDS

Business cards are a necessity. There is nothing worse than giving a potential customer your company information

DR. LAWN CARE
Landscaping

Joseph Public

123 Anystreet
Maryville, MI 48999   (313)555-4444

handwritten on a scrap piece of paper. A business card should have your company name, a brief description of what you do and a phone number where you can be reached. Never undervalue your business -- your customer will respect you for it.

113

SELLING CANDY

Selling candy is a great start in business for someone without a lot of money to invest. Both children and adults enjoy candy, and as a kid, you probably have a good idea of which candy items sell and which don't. You may also have experience selling candy through your church, school or community organization.

HOW TO GET STARTED

First, decide what candy you will sell. Choose items that are popular but not always available at nearby stores. Most brand name candies are available in different sizes and packages. If the neighborhood convenience store carries a regular candy bar for fifty cents, you may want to offer the same candy bar in a king-size version for eight-five cents.

Candy is one of the easiest products to buy wholesale. There was a time when only store owners could buy through select companies. However, with the emergence of membership warehouse clubs, it is easy for you to buy just about anything you need. Most membership clubs require that an adult join for $15 to $25 per year. Wholesale candy comes in large quantities, so be prepared to initially

invest anywhere from $10 to $30. You should also check your local yellow pages under "Candy - Wholesale," for other places to purchase your products.

Always monitor how much candy you sell on a daily or weekly basis. Keep a log of these numbers along with the total profit made. When all of your supply is sold, be sure to set aside enough money to replace or increase your inventory. There is nothing worse in business than a "stock out"-- when your customer expects to buy your product and you do not have it to sell.

MARKETING

Place family and friends at the top of your selling list. Classmates, before and after school, are great customers, too. They are always going to the store at these times and you will provide a great convenience for them.

PRICING

Once you have decided what you want to sell, you must set a price. You want to show a 100-200 percent mark-up on your product. That means if you buy your product at 10 cents, you want to sell it for 20 or even 30 cents. When you purchase candy wholesale, it comes in bulk -- 24, 48, or even 100 pieces. To find out how much you are paying per individual piece of candy, divide the amount of candy per box into the cost of the candy. For example, if you purchased a box which contained 48 pieces and you paid $3.50 for the box, you would use this equation to calculate the cost per piece:

3.50 divided by 48 = 0.072

Your individual pieces cost you 7 cents each. Therefore you should sell your candy at 15 or 20 cents a piece.

SNOW REMOVAL

If you are willing to work at various hours, are able to do hard work and don't mind cold weather, then snow removal may be a great source of income for you. No one really likes removing snow and you can take advantage of this great displeasure.

HOW TO GET STARTED

In the fall months, begin developing a list of potential customers. Pitch your upcoming service. Some people will commit right then, but also keep track of those who don't seem very interested. When the first big snow falls, they will probably need your services. So you may want to re-approach them.

Make sure you are dressed for working in cold temperatures. Pay special attention to your fingers and toes and keep in mind that snow removal is hard work. You must be physically prepared. Overworking yourself could be dangerous to your health, so work smart.

When shoveling, use your arms and knees to lift, not your back. Clear areas agreed upon by you and the customer. If there is ice under the snow, use your spade like a shovel to break it. Another option is to clear a little snow then cover the ice with salt. This process can be repeated and by the time you are done shoveling, the salt will have broken the ice so it can be removed more easily.

It is also a good idea to throw salt down after you have completed the job to avoid ice forming from the leftover water.

EQUIPMENT

Snow and Spade Shovel
Rock Salt or Ice Melter
Gloves, Boots, Hat and Thermal Underwear

MARKETING

Initially, decide who your customers are. Senior citizens and retirees are great potential customers. If you are aware of some seniors in your neighborhood, contact them first. Also, if you live near any businesses, especially high-traffic businesses like convenience stores or restaurants, let them know about your service. All businesses are required by law to keep sidewalks and walkways clear of snow and ice. Any slip and fall accidents could result in a negligence lawsuit. It wouldn't hurt for you to tactfully point this out on your flier by saying, for example, "Protect your business from careless injury - call us today." Business people are receptive to ideas that will save them money and time.

BUSINESS TIP

GOVERNMENT ASSISTANCE

Did you know that the state of Montana gives business loans to kids between the ages of 9 and 17? It's true! As long as you are a resident and want to start a business related to the agricultural industry, you can qualify. This program 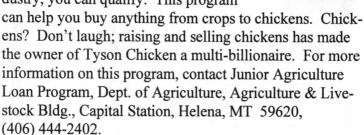 can help you buy anything from crops to chickens. Chickens? Don't laugh; raising and selling chickens has made the owner of Tyson Chicken a multi-billionaire. For more information on this program, contact Junior Agriculture Loan Program, Dept. of Agriculture, Agriculture & Livestock Bldg., Capital Station, Helena, MT 59620, (406) 444-2402.

For free information on government assistance regarding business plan development and management help for all minorities, contact U.S. Dept. of Commerce - Minority Business Agency at 14th and Constitution Ave. NW, Washington D.C. 20230, (202) 482-1936.

STANDARD JEWELRY MAKING

J ewelry making requires a little imagination and a lot of creativity, and if you possess both of these qualities, this venture could prove to be very successful.

HOW TO GET STARTED

Hand-crafted gemstone and beaded jewelry are very popular now and relatively inexpensive to start. Arts and crafts stores carry all the items you need for making jewelry, including beads, gemstones, earring clips, jewelry hooks, etc. If you are unfamiliar with this craft, it would be a good idea to pick up a "How-To" guide at an arts and crafts store. You may want to invest in a few pieces of already-made jewelry such as earrings, necklaces, and bracelets, to see how they are put together and to get more ideas. It will also give you an idea of the average cost of these items, so that you can set your own prices.

EQUIPMENT

Imitation Crystals and Gemstones	Glue
Earring Backings	Hooks and Catches
Beads and Fishing Wire	Backings for Pins

MARKETING

Begin with friends and family members; your best advertising comes from people wearing your creations, including yourself. When someone asks where you got that beautiful

bracelet or those gorgeous earrings, don't hesitate to tell
them; they are potential business. In addition, when your
mom, sisters and other adults wear your items to work or
school, this will surely keep the ball rolling. In the work-
place, there is always someone getting married, or people
who know of someone who's getting married. Weddings
are a great opportunity to sell many of your items at one
time. Often, the bride will want custom-made earrings
and/or necklaces for her bridesmaids. Advertising in other
places won't hurt, either. Many beauty salons have boutiques. Try selling directly to the salon owner or placing
your items there on a consignment basis. This could be a
great source of business, especially around the holidays.

Carl Jones and T.J. Walker

Cross Colours! Cross Colours! Cross Colours!

Brightly colored and uniquely-designed clothing, hats, and jackets have made Carl Jones and T.J. Walker the largest African-American apparel business in the United States. They began the company in 1990, and in the first year of business recorded $115 million in sales. What makes Cross Colours a valuable entity in the African-American community is not only its economic success, but its socially responsible message of non-violence, equality, cooperative economics and unity.

VIDEO CAMCORDER RECORDING

Do you or your parents own a video camcorder? Well, perhaps they will either loan or rent it to you to earn income for yourself. There are many ways to make money with a video camcorder, but let's consider ways that will not require a lot of extra equipment and help. For instance, how about videotaping individuals taking lessons for such things as golfing, tennis, bowling and the like. Also, how about a relative's up-coming graduation. With a regular video camera and an inventive marketing plan, video camcorder recording could be a very profitable past time.

HOW TO GET STARTED

First, become familiar with your equipment. Most camcorder owners do not completely read the manufactures instructions, which can enable you to use the full potential of your camera. Once you become familiar with your equipment, pick up a basic videotaping technique book from your local library or bookstore. This type of book should have tips on everything from editing to lighting. Practice around the house. Using your camera to shoot different ob-

jects and at different times of the day, should greatly improve your videotaping skills.

EQUIPMENT

Camcorder
Tripod
VCR and Television or Monitor
Blank Videotapes, Cases and Labels
Extra Battery Pack
Long Heavy Duty Extension Cord
Carrying Case

MARKETING

Begin locally, by placing fliers detailing your video camcorder service in libraries, local schools, golf courses, bowling alleys, and the like with their permission. Ask the coach at school or the principal if they would be interested in having you record the team's practice sessions to review. Videotapes can help people improve themselves, whether they are practicing debates or handstands. Also, insurance companies accept video proof of residential and business contents for insurance claims. All you have to do is take your camera to businesses and residences to provide the customer with a tape of the contents. Contact business and home insurance agencies to offer your service to their customers. Keep track of upcoming local events and celebrations, such as birthday parties, graduations and weddings. Parents love the idea of preserving the memory of their child's first birthday. However, most people, even camcorder owners, don't want to spend this treasured time videotaping.

You may want to offer to produce a back-up copy of their tape, that you will keep on file at no additional charge (several customers can be kept on one tape if you record in the EP or SLP speed mode) for the first year. After the first year, you can charge an annual storage fee to keep a back-up copy for the insurance company or the policy holder to review if an insurance claim is made for an item on the videotape.

When a customer wishes you to videotape items for insurance purposes, it will be important to send reminders to them letting them know it may be time to update their tape for new items. You can update it for a reasonable rate. The nice thing about updating is that you can add it to your customer's existing tape through editing. Be creative with bonuses and giveaways for your customers. For example, if they have a VCR, give them a free blank tape along with a business card. Don't forget to get your own customized T-shirts and caps printed for promotions.

PRICING

Find out what your competitors are charging. However, it is important to determine how long it will take you to tape and whether editing is required. Include the cost of labor (the amount of time it takes times the hourly rate you want to pay yourself). For example, if it takes 2 hours to videotape a project and your hourly rate is $10, then the cost of labor is $20. In addition, you must factor in the cost of tapes and materials. For instance, a $25 fee to tape the contents of either a home or small office might be appropriate. If the job takes less than an hour and the tape cost you $5--guess what?--you have just made $20 per hour!

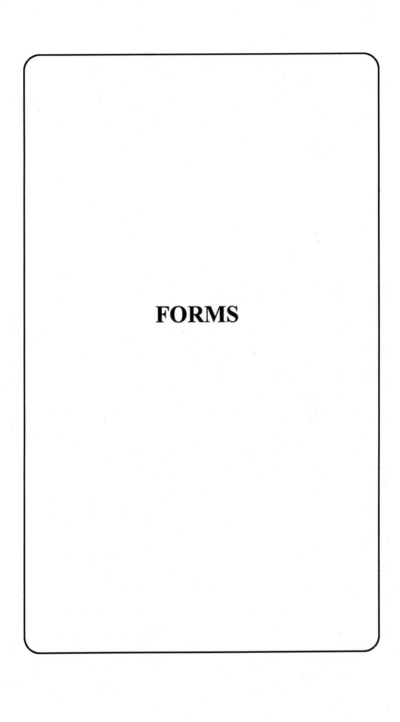

FORMS

A *Purchase Order* is a document used to keep track of the goods and supplies you purchase. It is a good idea to fill one out each time you buy an item for business. This will be helpful for your records and to control spending.

		Purchase Order#:		
		PURCHASE ORDER		
VENDOR:		Ship To:		

	Quantity	Description	Price	Amount
1.				
2.				
3.				
4.				
5.				
6.				
7.				
8.				
9.				
10.				
11.				
12.				

If you handle resaleable goods and supplies, it is a good idea to use an *Inventory Log*, which will tell you exactly how much product you have on hand, and where it is.

INVENTORY RECORD		Date:			
Department			Sheet	Of	
Location					
Stock#	Description	Qty.	Unit	Price	Total $

An *Invoice* is used to keep a record of money you have
made. It also acts as a receipt for your customer. It is a
common practice to give your customer a copy of an invoice after they have purchased goods or service from you.

INVOICE

| INVOICE #: | P.O. #: |

| SOLD TO | SHIP TO |

Qty Ordered	Qty Shipped	Description	Price	Total

| | | | Subtotal | |
| | | | Sales Tax | |

| DATE | SALESPERSON | Total | |

Income Journals are used to record all sales and income for each month of the year. Log the date, invoice number and customer name for each transaction that brings income into your business. Total all income at the end of the month and transfer that amount to the income field on your Profit and Loss Statement.

INCOME JOURNAL

MONTH / YEAR _____ / _____

Date	Invoice # / Customer	Amount
	Total	

Expense Journals are used to record and keep track of all your expenses for a particular month. Log the date, purchase order number and purpose of each business item or service you buy or pay for. Total all expenses at the end of the month and transfer that amount to the expense field on your Profit and Loss Statement.

EXPENSE JOURNAL

MONTH / YEAR _____ / _____

Date	Purchase Order # / Purpose	Amount
	Total	

A *Profit & Loss Statement* shows if a business is making or losing money. Use this form to record all expenses and income for a particular month. If your income is more than your expenses, then you are profitable. If your expenses exceed your income then you are at a loss. You always want to make a profit!

PROFIT & LOSS STATEMENT

MONTH / YEAR _____ / _____

Total Income   _____

Total Expenses   _____

Profit or (Loss)   _____

Packing Slips are used when sending or delivering goods you have sold to a customer. This document is attached to the package and tells the customer exactly what is inside.

PACKING SLIP

Contact: [_____]   P.O. #: [_____]

SOLD TO	SHIP TO
_____	_____
_____	_____
_____	_____
_____	_____

Product #	Qty	Description	Price	Amount	Discount	Total

Terms and Conditions

Subtotal	
Sales Tax	
Total	

Weight :_____   Filled By :_____

No. of Pieces :_____   Checked By : _____

Date Shipped :_____   Delivered By : _____

Monthly Planners are a great way to schedule any business or personal commitments you may have. It is a good idea to plan events early on, especially if your business depends on holidays or seasons.

Monthly Activity Planner

Month: _____ **Year:** _____

	DATE:	DATE:	DATE:
M O N D A Y			
T U E S D A Y	DATE:	DATE:	DATE:
W E D N E S D A Y	DATE:	DATE:	DATE:
T H U R S D A Y	DATE:	DATE:	DATE:
F R I D A Y	DATE:	DATE:	DATE:
S A T U R D A Y	DATE:	DATE:	DATE:
S U N D A Y	DATE:	DATE:	DATE:

Daily Planners are perfect for keeping track of appointments you've made through out the day. It is a good practice not to overload your daily commitments. You want to give yourself ample time to complete any jobs or appointments you may have.

DAILY   PLANNER

FOR:

8:00 - 9:00	
9:00 - 10:00	
10:00 - 11:00	
11:00 - 12:00	
12:00 - 1:00	
1:00 - 2:00	
2:00 - 3:00	
3:00 - 4:00	
4:00 - 5:00	
5:00 - 6:00	
6:00 - 7:00	
7:00 - 8:00	
8:00 - 9:00	
9:00 - 10:00	

Pleasant   dreams.

A *Things To Do* list will remind you of certain responsibilities you have to perform at home or for your business. From homework to filing your business invoices, this form can help you complete your day to day duties.

Things To Do

Date

1
2
3
4
5
6
7
8
9
10
11
12

GLOSSARY

Accounts Payable
Unpaid bills from buying goods and services.

Accounts Receivable
Uncollected money owed to a company for providing goods and services.

Accrual Basis
The practice of recording a sale when it actually happens instead of when the actual cash is received. This accounting practice is used mostly by large corporations.

Accrued
The interest earned from reinvesting in a present account.

Action Plan
A plan for the purpose of reaching a particular goal in a certain amount of time.

Advertise
To inform the public of goods and services you offer; can be done with fliers, signs, media ads.

Agreement
A mutual understanding between two or more individuals on particular terms of a deal.

Asset
An item that can be converted into cash.

Balance Sheet
An accounting document to show the assets, liabilities, and net worth of a business at a certain time.

Balancing the Budget
Keeping the amount of money spent less than the amount made.

Bargain
An item purchased for less than the regular price.

Bazaar
A function put together by an organization to raise money by renting booths or tables to merchants for the sale goods to the public.

Benefits
The extra perks given to an employee such as health insurance, retirement plans, expense accounts, etc.

Blue Chip
Strong stocks from companies known for stability and fairly consistent profitable performance.

Bonds
A certificate of ownership from a corporation or government that pays interest.

Break Even
When a companies sales equals its costs.

Brochure
A small booklet, usually one to two sheets, used by a company to inform a potential customer of their goods and services.

Budget
A plan for spending the money you earn.

Business
An entity put together to gain profit by selling goods or services.

Business Plan
A written plan that describes the idea for a business, the organizational structure and projections for the future.

Capital
The money one has to invest.

Capital Gain
The money one makes from selling an asset.

Cash Basis
The practice of recording a sale only when the cash is received. This accounting practice is usually used by small businesses.

Cash Flow
Maintaining a consistent flow of cash to a business by keeping a company's sells up at the same time managing to keep debts owed to the business at a minimum.

Collateral
Assets put up by a borrower to secure a loan.

C.O.D.
"Collect on delivery" is a term used to let a customer know that all money is due when goods are delivered or services are completed.

Common Stock
Shares that represent ownership in a company.

Consignment
To leave merchandise with a business with the ideal of them selling it to their current clientele. You are paid when the merchandise is sold. The business keeps a portion of the money for selling the product (usually 30%).

Consumer
The person who purchases goods and services for personal needs.

Corporation
A business structure where stockholders own the company and share profits with limited liability.

Cost of Goods
The monetary value of the inventory a company sells.

Co-workers
People who work together.

Credit
To attain goods and services without immediate payment.

Customers
The people who buy your products or services.

Debit
To record a debt to an account.

Demand
The consumer's desire for and power to purchase a product.

Demographics
Profiling a customer or potential customer by age, sex, income, occupation, etc.

Depreciation
A decrease in an assets' value due to wear, usage and decline in price.

Diversification
To manufacture, invest in or sell different types of merchandise or services.

Dividend
The portion of profits paid to shareholders of a corporation.

Door-to Door
The act of going from house to house or business to business to sell a product or service.

Dun & Bradstreet
A private corporation that rates and reports a company's history and stability to other companies for a fee.

Entrepreneur
A person who creates, organizes and runs a business venture.

Equity
The value of a property or business after all liabilities are satisfied.

Estimate
A rough calculation of how much a certain job or product will cost your customer.

Fad
A passing style that will be popular for a short period.

Fixed Expenses
Expenses unrelated to the sales performance of a business, such as rent or insurance.

Flea Market
A place where inexpensive and second-hand items are sold.

Flier
A single sheet of paper with information advertising a business or service.

General Partner
A managing partner with substantial ownership and unlimited liability. (see "Limited Partner" for comparison)

Going Rate
The standard amount of pay acceptable for a certain job or service.

Gross Profit
Profit after cost of goods sold but before expenses.

Gross National Product
The complete monetary value of goods and services of a country in one year.

Hire
Agreeing to pay a person for a certain task.

Intangible Asset
Assets not visible and cannot be given monetary value.

Interest
The money you earn from an investment.

Inventory
The merchandise you have on hand to sale.

Invest
To risk a certain amount of money or time for potential profit.

Invoice
A document used by businesses for billing goods and services.

Leverage
The act of putting up assets to secure loans for the purpose of investing in another asset with the potential of higher return.

Liability
Debts owed.

Limited Partner
An partner with limited liability and no managing rights.

Liquid
Assets that are cash or can be easily converted into cash.

Load
The commission charged to an investor by a stock brokerage firm.

Market Value
The price or value that your business or property is worth on the open market.

Marketing
The means you use to get your customer and promote your business.

Monopoly
A company that controls and dominates the market for a particular product.

Mutual Funds
When brokerage houses use the cash from many investors to invest in the stock of many different companies.

Net
Cash left when all expenses are paid.

Net 30
A payment agreement where a customer agrees to pay a vendor for goods or services 30 days after receiving them.

Networking
The act of establishing business relationships through friends and associates.

Net Worth
The value of a business or individual after liabilities.

Niche
A unique service or product that sets a company apart from the competition.

Oligopoly
Market conditions that exist when there are only a few sellers.

Opportunity
A favorable time to achieve something with little chance of failure.

Overhead
The general cost of running a business; fixed expenses.

On-Call
When one is available to a customer for services whenever they need you.

Portfolio
A complete assessment of an individual or company's assets.

Preferred Stock
Stock that has rights to dividends before shareholders of common stock.

Price List
A list of the dollar amount you expect to be paid for a particular product or service.

Product
The items you make or buy to sell for profit.

Profit
The amount of money remaining after a business pays its expenses.

Purchase Order
A form used to record the purchase of goods and services.

Retail
A business that sells goods to the consumer.

Royalty
Compensation paid to artist, composers, authors, inventors, entertainers, etc. for the use of their goods, services or likeness.

Salesperson
A person who earns money by selling products or services.

Self-Employed
A person who makes a living from owning a business.

Service
Labor based work with a minimal use of supplies.

Sole Proprietorship
A business structure where there is one owner who assumes all the profit and liability(debts).

Split
To divide outstanding stock usually to benefit current shareholders.

Stationery
Business paper and envelopes used for writing or typing, usually with the company name and address printed.

Stock-Outs
When a business does not have certain goods to sell due to poor inventory control.

Supplier
A business that sells products directly to other businesses rather than selling to the consumer.

Supply
The quantity of a product on hand.

Tangible Assets
Physical assets that can be given monetary value.

Target Customer
The person you believe will need or want your goods or services.

Trademark
A registered icon or symbol that reminds people of a particular business or product.

Trade References
Vendors or suppliers that can vouch for a company's existence and credit history.

Transaction
The activity of buying or selling goods and services between two parties.

Variable Expenses
Expense directly attributed to sales performance.

Vendor
A business that sells goods and services to other businesses.

Wholesale
Goods purchased in large quantities at a discount .

Word of Mouth
When satisfied customers tell others about your business, product, services, etc.

Yield
The amount of profit from an investment.

Registration

Please complete this form. Registration will put your name on our business database for future mailings. It is our intention to keep in contact with our readers to provide notice of any programs or literature that may benefit their current or future businesses. Send to: Xpression Publishing, 453 MLK Blvd., Detroit, MI 48201

Reader's Name: _____

Parents: _____

Address: _____

City: _____ State/Province: _____

Zip/Postal Code: _____ Country: _____

Business Interest: _____

Comments: _____

_____

_____

To Schools, Non-Profits and Corporations

For information on training courses and bulk discounts regarding this book.
Write to: Xpression Publishing, 453 MLK Blvd.,
Detroit, MI 48201 or Call (313) 833-0633

INDEX